It's Laugh

Would You Rather?

Trick-or-Treat Edition

Funny Scenarios, Wacky Choices and Hilarious Situations For Kids and Family

With Fun Illustrations

Riddleland

Designs by freepik.com

TABLE OF CONTENTS

Riddleland Bonus

Join our **Facebook Group** at **Riddleland for Kids** to get daily jokes and riddles.

https://pixelfy.me/riddlelandbonus

Thank you for buying this book. As a token of our appreciation, we would like to offer a special bonus—a collection of 50 original jokes, riddles, and funny stories.

INTRODUCTION

"During the day, I don't believe in ghosts. At night, I'm a little more open-minded."

~ Unknown

Are you ready to make some decisions? ***Would You Rather? Trick or Treat Edition*** is a collection of funny scenarios, wacky choices, and hilarious situations which offer alternative endings for kids and adults to choose among.

These questions are an excellent way to get a fun and exciting conversation started. Also, by asking "Why?" after a "Would you Rather . . . " question, learn a lot about the person, including their values and their thinking process.

We wrote this book because we want children to be encouraged to read more, think, and grow. As parents, we know that when children play games, they are being educated while having so much fun that they don't even realize they're learning and developing valuable life skills. "Would you Rather . . . " is one of our favorite games to play as a family. Some of the 'would you rather ...' scenarios have had us in fits of giggles, others have generated reactions such as: "Eeeeeeuuugh, that's gross!" and yet others really make us think, reflect and consider our own decisions.

Besides having fun, playing these questions have other benefits such as:

Enhancing Communication – This game helps children to interact, read aloud, and listen to others. It's a fun way for parents to get their children interacting with them without a formal, awkward conversation. The game can also help to get to know someone better and learn about their likes, dislikes, and values.

Building Confidence – The game encourages children to get used to pronouncing vocabulary, asking questions, and overcoming shyness.

Developing Critical Thinking – It helps children to defend and justify the rationale for their choices and can generate discussions and debates. Parents playing this game with young children can give them prompting questions about their answers to help them reach logical and sensible decisions.

Improving Vocabulary – Children will be introduced to new words in the questions, and the context of them will help them remember the words because the game is fun.

Encouraging Equality and Diversity – Considering other people's answers, even if they differ from your own, is important for respect, equality, diversity, tolerance, acceptance, and inclusivity. Some questions may get children to think outside the box and move beyond stereotypes associated with gender.

Welcome to It's Laugh O'Clock

Would You Rather?

Trick-or-Treat Edition

How do you play?

At least two players are needed to play this game. Face your opponent and decide who is **Spooky Ghost 1** and **Spooky Ghost 2**. If you have 3 or 4 players, you can decide which players belong to **Spooky Group 1** and **Spooky Group 2**. The goal of the game is to score points by making the other players laugh. The first player to a score of 10 points is the **Champion**.

What are the rules?

Spooky Ghost 1 starts first. Read the questions aloud and choose an answer. The same player will then explain why they chose the answer in the silliest and wackiest way possible. If the reason makes the Spooky Ghost 2 laugh, then Spooky Ghost 1 scores a funny point. Take turns going back and forth and write down the score.

If you have three or four players

Flip a coin. The player that guesses it correctly starts first.

Bonus Tip:

Making funny voices, silly dance moves or wacky facial expressions will make your opponent laugh!

Most Importantly:

Remember to have fun and enjoy the game!

Would You Rather...

Play kickball with Frankenstein's monster who can only grunt to talk

with a ghost who can disappear on the field at any moment?

Walk through a spooky corn maze all by yourself with a treasure chest full of candy at the end

have a sleepover with your best friend in a haunted house made of chocolate?

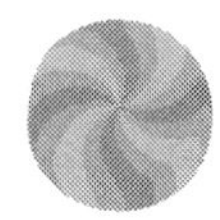

Would You Rather...

Drink a witch's potion that gives you the power to extend your bedtime by one hour every night

that gives you the power to make animals talk in human voices?

Take a field trip to a blood bank with a dancing vampire

to an ancient-Egyptian museum with a singing mummy?

Would You Rather...

Join a monster rock band to play drums made from pumpkins

to play a keyboard made from skeleton bones?

Build a treehouse in the jungle for a black cat who likes to make costumes

an underground bunker in the desert for a vampire who likes to make candy?

Would You Rather...

Grow up to be a hairstylist who braids werewolf hair

a dentist who cleans vampire teeth?

Hike a mountain where hungry werewolves live to get the biggest piece of candy in the world

go to your best friend's house to have a monster dinner party where broccoli is the main course?

Would You Rather...

Eat a Halloween cupcake made from creamy, gooey goblin eyeballs

made from long, pointy dragon toenails?

Go trick-or-treating under the sea with a pod of dolphins who dress up like dinosaurs

in outer space with aliens who dress up like human celebrities?

Would You Rather...

Sing the alphabet while taking a bubble bath with a howling werewolf

while hanging upside-down in your closet with a screeching bat?

Compete in a race as a mummy who walks slowly but with great big steps

as a spider who crawls quickly but with teeny tiny legs?

Would You Rather...

Learn a spell that turns zombies back into humans

that turns vegetables into candy?

Go trick-or-treating in an enchanted forest guarded by giant spiders who will only let you pass if you give them some of your candy

in a magic cloud castle guarded by knights who will only let you pass if you tell jokes?

Would You Rather...

Go on a beach vacation with a witch who's afraid of the water

with a ghost who sunburns easily?

Have an enchanted treat bag that feels weightless, no matter how much candy you put in it

magic shoes that keep your feet from getting tired, no matter how much trick-or-treating you do?

Would You Rather...

Have a tarantula who lays candy eggs as your class pet

an owl who likes to dress up in costumes as your class pet?

Go trick-or-treating at a haunted house located in the jungle that's made out of twisty tree vines

at a spooky castle located in the desert that's made out of spiky cactus thorns?

Would You Rather...

Go camping with Frankenstein's monster
who packed ingredients for s'mores

with a ghost who brought a canteen full of hot chocolate?

Hide your Halloween candy in a booby-trapped treasure
chest at the bottom of the Pacific Ocean

in a combination-locked safe at
the top of Mount Everest?

Would You Rather...

Bake a 12-layer wedding cake for the Bride of Frankenstein

build coffin bunk beds for Count Dracula?

Go to a Halloween party where the guests dress as dinosaurs and compete in a disco dance contest

dress as monsters and compete in a cookie baking contest?

Would You Rather...

Go to the movies with a zombie who eats most of your popcorn

with a mad scientist who slurps loudly on soda?

Use a time machine to go trick-or-treating in the past with a dinosaur in an ancient jungle

in the future with an alien in a newly discovered galaxy?

Would You Rather...

Host a Halloween party at your school for a colony of aliens

go to a Halloween party in a spaceship with experienced astronauts?

Take a class where Dr. Frankenstein teaches you how to speak German

where Count Dracula teaches you how to do algebra?

Would You Rather...

Take care of a howling werewolf pup with a mohawk in its fur

a hungry vampire baby with broccoli in its teeth?

Get an extra candy bag by walking through a cemetery full of zombies

a haunted house full of sticky spiderwebs full of dead bugs?

Would You Rather...

Eat all your Halloween candy with a devil's pitchfork

with the spoon from a witch's cauldron?

Cast a magic spell on your neighbors that made them think Halloween was three nights in a row so you could go trick-or-treating three times

that made them only buy king-sized candy bars to give to all the trick-or-treaters?

Would You Rather...

Dress up as an astronaut in a tie-dyed space suit

as a mad scientist in a polka-dotted lab coat?

Cast a spell on Halloween night that makes the Statue of Liberty come to life and go trick-or-treating

that made the Mount Rushmore presidents come to life and take funny selfies with monument visitors?

Would You Rather...

Have your Halloween candy protected by a family of invisible ninjas

by a terrifying, three-headed dragon?

Have a magic mirror that tells you how good you look in your costume

that tells you where to find the best candy in your neighborhood?

Would You Rather...

Drive a monster truck that has
pumpkin tires

fly an airplane that has bat wings?

Would you rather go trick-or-treating in a neighborhood
that has sidewalks made from water that you sail
on in a Viking ship to get to the next house

that has sidewalks with zip line ropes that you ride
on to get to the next house?

Would You Rather...

Fly a broomstick with
a jet pack

drive a race car made from a vampire's coffin?

Have a wizard turn you into a blue whale that goes
trick-or-treating for licorice-flavored krill

a flying squirrel that goes trick-or-treating for gummy
bear-flavored acorns?

Would You Rather...

Plant a magic garden full of pumpkins that grow into pumpkin pie

plant corn that grows into caramel popcorn?

Go trick-or-treating with a monkey who eats a piece of your candy whenever you're not looking

with a duck who tells bad jokes to all of your friends?

Would You Rather...

Have a dog who eats skeleton bones

a chicken who eats candy corn?

Have a ghost pepper eating contest with the Grim Reaper at a barbecue in your backyard

have a pumpkin spice milkshake drinking contest with your best friend at a diner named the Haunted Hamburger?

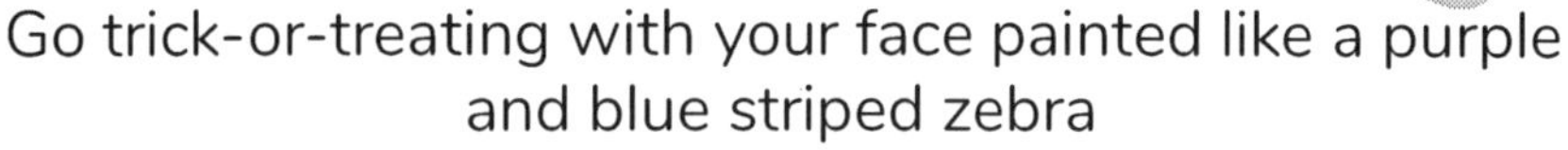

Would You Rather...

Go trick-or-treating with your face painted like a purple and blue striped zebra

like a red and pink spotted giraffe?

Read a blog about how to make giant, diaper-wearing baby costumes for your family

about how to get super-sized chocolate bars with rainbow sprinkles for your class?

Would You Rather...

Eat a creamy chocolate bar that gives you garlic breath to ward off vampires

that gives you fire breath to scare witches away?

Demolish a haunted house at night by blasting it with sparkly orange fireworks

by crushing it with a glow-in-the-dark bulldozer?

Would You Rather...

Carve a jack-o-lantern face into a small, slippery spaghetti squash

into a big, juicy watermelon?

Have a sports announcer follow you around while you go trick-or-treating and explain everything you do

have a marching band walk alongside you and play a song every time you collect a piece of candy?

Would You Rather...

Drink steamy apple cider that gives you the power to fill your treat bag instantly

a bubbly hot chocolate that gives you the power to turn little candy bars into big ones?

Do a TikTok video dressed up as a unicorn who likes to breakdance

as a superhero who likes to do ballet?

Ride your bike through a spooky corn maze with glow-in-the-dark spiders

through a haunted forest with talking trees?

Find in your treat bag, enchanted sidewalk chalk that makes your pictures come to life

a deck of cards that instantly teaches you magic tricks?

Would You Rather...

Go to a carnival to ride a loopy rollercoaster with a wizard

ride in spinning bumper cars with a goblin?

Go trick-or-treating with a black cat that meows whenever someone says "trick-or-treat"

with a werewolf that howls every time someone says "candy?"

Watch video tutorials about making a magnetic costume that attracts candy

about making a magic potion that gives you the ability to fly on Halloween night?

Have a costume fashion show with your class where everyone dresses up in sparkly ninja outfits

metallic princess dresses?

Would You Rather...

Go to a Halloween party dressed as a clown who juggles mangoes

OR

as a martial arts champion who karate chops tacos?

Go trick-or-treating while crawling on your hands and knees like a baby

OR

while walking on your hands like an acrobat?

Would You Rather...

Wear Halloween pajamas all year long

wear your costume backward to school
for one whole day?

Watch the evening news with newscasters who turn into different monsters after every commercial break

a detective show with a vampire police officer who can turn into a bat to spy on criminals?

Would You Rather...

Get an extra candy bucket by swimming to the bottom of the ocean dressed as a shark wearing a hat on its dorsal fin

by climbing a tall palm tree dressed as a monkey wearing a scrunchie on its tail?

Eat a bowl of candy corn that gives you stinky garlic breath

bob for apples that taste like jalapeños?

Would You Rather...

See an elephant dressed up on Halloween
as your favorite celebrity wearing a cowboy hat

your favorite cartoon character wearing high heels?

Volunteer to take care of a colony of hungry bats
who live in a haunted tunnel

to take care of a litter of sleepy black cats
who live in a spooky treehouse?

Would You Rather...

Let a creepy, yellow spider crawl on your neck

a slimy, pink snake slither around your legs?

Go trick-or-treating in a neighborhood that has sidewalks made from bouncy trampolines that you jump on to get to the next house

made from wooden skateboard ramps that you skate on to get to the next house?

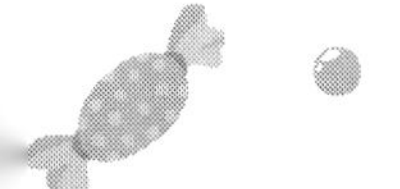

Would You Rather...

Jump into a swimming pool full of crunchy fall leaves

jump on the tops of pumpkins that bounce like trampolines?

Go trick-or-treating in China dressed as a panda wearing oven mitts

in Australia dressed as a kangaroo wearing snow boots?

Would You Rather...

Have a witch cast a spell that turned you into
a robot who likes to surf

an alien who likes to jet ski?

Drive a haunted food truck that serves barbecued
skeleton ribs and candy corn on the cob

that served Transylvanian tacos and
bat burritos?

Would You Rather...

Moo like a cow instead of saying "trick-or-treat"

cluck like a chicken every time you eat a piece of candy?

Go trick-or-treating dressed as a giant hot dog

stay home and hand out candy dressed as a rainbow-colored bubble gum machine?

Would You Rather...

Train a chihuahua to sniff out houses that have your favorite treats

train a bulldog to fetch your candy bag every time you want to eat a piece?

Dress up as an octopus that grabs candy with its eight, slimy tentacles

as a pelican that scoops candy with a big, shovel-like beak?

Roll down a grassy hill in a puffy sumo wrestler costume

play a racing arcade game with one hand in a tiny-armed Tyrannnosaurus rex costume

Go trick-or-treating on a sandy beach with a flamingo wearing heart-shaped sunglasses

on a snowy mountain with a buffalo wearing rhinestone cowboy boots?

Would You Rather...

Trade your candy for an extra-large pizza with pepperoni and spider legs

a double-decker cheeseburger with crispy bat toenails?

Find a magic wand that gives you the power to eat pancakes for dinner with a swamp creature

to eat macaroni and cheese for breakfast with a fortune-teller?

Would You Rather...

Share a candy corn-flavored milkshake with a thirsty goblin

a bubblegum-flavored muffin with a hungry wizard?

Get dropped off at a zombie's Halloween party in a blue helicopter

at a ghost's Halloween party in an orange tractor?

Would You Rather...

Shop for bat food at the grocery store with a coffin-shaped shopping cart

for witch hats at the party supply store with a cauldron-shaped handle basket?

Go trick-or-treating with a superhero who wears a purple polka dot cape

with a monster who wears a green glittery cowboy hat?

Drink a mystical potion that makes you burp fire

hiccup bubbles?

Drink magic apple cider out of a sippy cup that gives you the ability to walk on the ceiling

drink an enchanted hot chocolate out of a cup with a twisty straw that gives you the ability to walk on water?

Would You Rather...

Dress up like a Hawaiian hula dancer and get pineapples in your treat bag

dress up like a Parisian poodle and get French toast in your treat bag?

Trade your favorite lunch for a grilled cheese and candy corn sandwich

a peanut butter and purple slime sandwich?

Would You Rather...

Go trick-or-treating for jelly donuts that smell like Frankenstein's burps

for cookie dough milkshakes that smell like a dragon's feet?

Host a sleepover where everyone sleeps in coffins

a swimming party where everyone dries off with towels made from mummy bandages?

Would You Rather...

Read a book about a pirate ship with a zombie crew that likes to tell jokes

make up your own ghost story about a haunted castle with an evil spider queen?

Dress up as a cowboy with a revolver that shoots cotton candy bubbles

as an alien with a blaster that shoots licorice laser beams?

Would You Rather...

Have a pillow fight in a fancy hotel room with a monster who lives under the bed

in a haunted cabin with a vampire bat who lives in the attic?

Work in a costume shop owned by a zombie who only wears tuxedos

in a candy shop run by human-sized gummy bears?

Would You Rather...

Use toilet paper made from mummy bandages

a hairbrush made from vampire teeth?

Learn a spell on Halloween night that gives you the ability to teleport to different neighborhoods all around the world

that gives you the power to snap your fingers to instantly change your costume as many times as you want?

Would You Rather...

Drink a witch's potion made from pumpkin pie, frog warts, and hot sauce

made from caramel corn, newt eyes, and ranch dressing?

Have a wizard teach you a spell that gets someone else to do your chores for you

that gives you an extra hour of screen time every day?

Would You Rather...

Go bowling with a pumpkin as your bowling ball

play mini golf with a broomstick as your golf club?

Spend Halloween with a kid your age who's never been trick-or-treating before and wants to dress up like a giant banana

with a kid your age who's never seen a Halloween movie before and wants to dress up like a goofy balloon animal?

Would You Rather...

Have a Zoom meeting with a class of monsters who are counting candy in a jar

a class of goblins who are reading spooky stories to the teacher?

Take school pictures with a noticeable piece of candy corn stuck in your teeth

with a tuft of werewolf fur sticking out of each of your ears?

Would You Rather...

Do a Halloween photoshoot with your friends dressed as aliens wearing tutus

as ninjas wearing cargo pants?

Find a magic wand that summons friendly spiders to clean your room

that makes a mad scientist appear to do all your homework?

Would You Rather...

Dress up as a vampire wearing
a leopard-print cape

as a mummy wearing camouflage-print bandages?

Ride on a Halloween parade float decorated with black roses and toss king-size candy bars to onlookers

on a parade float decorated with purple tarantulas and launch fireworks that sprinkle confetti when they explode?

Would You Rather...

Eat a piece of candy that makes you grow frog warts on your tongue

newt eyes on your fingers?

Go to a Halloween concert and crowd surf over an audience of zombies who listen to rap music

get pulled up on stage to sing with a band of werewolves who play country music?

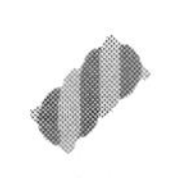

Would You Rather...

Sneak your teacher a magic potion that makes them give you good grades on all your homework

that lets you go to recess early every day?

Go trick-or-treating during a flood and get from house to house in a kayak

during a windstorm and get from house to house in a parachute?

Would You Rather...

Wear a fancy suit to have a mud fight with a swamp monster

ballerina slippers to have a snowball fight with Bigfoot?

Find in your treat bag a magic ticket that lets you cut to the front of the school lunch line

an enchanted coin that lets you sit next to your best friend in class?

Would You Rather...

Play hopscotch with a creepy doll in a pumpkin patch

ride bikes with a scary clown through a corn maze?

Have to unwrap your Halloween candy dressed as a sea creature with pinchy lobster claws

as a unicorn with slippery horseshoes?

Would You Rather...

Dress up as a black cat and have to yell,
"I'm a floofy kitty," at every house you go to

dress up like a superhero and have to say, "Captain Booger is here to save the day," every time you eat

Sing the "Monster Mash" to baby ogres

"I Put a Spell on You" to teenage witches?

Make your own robot costume with a built-in candy magnet to get extra treats

buy a ninja costume that comes with nunchucks made from garlic to ward off vampires?

Ride on the back of a black cat wearing roller-skates

on the back of a bat wearing a jet engine?

Would You Rather...

See your teacher turn into a werewolf and howl at the moon

your principal turn into a vampire bat and fly over the school?

Grow up to be a real estate agent who sells haunted houses to monster families

a physical therapist who works on skeletons with knee injuries?

Would You Rather...

Go to a haunted football game where the players are skeletons who fall apart every time they're tackled

where the fans are ghosts who say "boo" even when their team wins?

Go trick-or-treating as a magician with dreadlocks that touch the ground

as a farmer with a tall, spiky mohawk?

Would You Rather...

Go trick-or-treating on Easter and collect Easter eggs with candy corn inside

on Christmas and collect Christmas cookies with pumpkin-flavored frosting?

Keep your candy safe in a sludgy bayou guarded by swamp creatures

in a fiery volcano guarded by lava monsters?

Would You Rather...

Wear a monkey costume and have to unwrap candy while waving your arms over your head

wear a dinosaur costume and unwrap candy with your teeny tiny T. rex arms?

Go trick-or-treating with a mummy wearing a pink leather jacket

with a ghost wearing a fuzzy yellow bathrobe?

Would You Rather...

Read a Halloween fantasy book about trolls who go trick-or-treating in the forest

a Halloween sci-fi book about aliens who wear costumes to look like earthlings?

Clean a kitchen full of 100 slimy witch cauldrons

vacuum a haunted mansion full of 1,000 sticky spiderwebs?

Would You Rather...

Spend Halloween day gardening carnivorous Venus flytrap plants in your backyard

at a bowling alley with a league of werewolves who use pumpkins instead of bowling balls?

Shave a werewolf's armpits with a buzzing electric trimmer

style a wizard's beard with drippy candle wax?

Would You Rather...

Be a barista at a coffee shop that brews magic potion lattes that make trick-or-treaters fly

a chef at a restaurant who bakes pumpkin pies that make people turn into werewolves?

Go trick-or-treating in a speed boat on the Amazon River

in a dog sled on a giant iceberg in Antarctica?

Would You Rather...

Dress as Frankenstein's monster with neck bolts made out of chopsticks

as a pirate with an eye patch made out of a maple leaf?

Go to a Halloween beauty conference to watch scary clowns apply their makeup

go to a haunted racetrack to watch fuzzy spiders ride in remote control race cars?

Would You Rather...

Go trick-or-treating dressed as a flamingo
who likes to rap

as a penguin who likes to yodel?

Go on a Halloween road trip and play “I spy” with
a cyclops who reads too much and gets car sick

play “20 questions” with a mutant who drinks too much
soda and has to pull over to go to the bathroom?

Would You Rather...

Dress up as a unicorn who wears sparkly, polka-dotted headphones and likes to DJ

as a llama who wears fuzzy, leopard print army boots and likes to sing?

Join a choir of monsters who like to sing nursery rhymes

a symphony of zombies who like to play pop songs?

Would You Rather...

Drink a witch's brew that lets you eat as much candy as you want without getting a tummy ache

that extends Halloween to two nights so you can go trick-or-treating twice?

Look in a fortune teller's crystal ball and see a horse riding a cowboy

a bull charging at a matador?

Have a slumber party with a black cat
who likes to snore

a werewolf pup who likes to hog the bed?

Visit a haunted aquarium during feeding time to watch a giant squid eat a pirate ship with a pink skull and crossbones flag

to watch a polka-dotted sea serpent eat a crunchy seaweed salad?

Would You Rather...

Play hopscotch dressed like a fluffy bunny with vampire fangs

have a water balloon fight dressed like a baseball player with T. rex arms?

Visit a Halloween Renaissance fair to have a zombie knight teach you how to joust with a giant piece of licorice

have a werewolf archer teach you how to hit targets with candy corn arrows?

Would You Rather...

Dress up like a cyborg wearing sparkly bracelets all the way up your arms

an elephant wearing dangly earrings that hang all the way to the floor?

Tour an enchanted candy shop where gummy bears come to life and make the candy

a magic costume shop for pets where black cats walk like humans and model costumes?

Would You Rather...

Take a selfie with a filter that gives you glittery, green demon horns

a neon yellow witch hat?

Travel to France on Halloween to have gargoyles from the Notre Dame Cathedral come to life and teach you how to fly

have the Mona Lisa magically jump out of her painting and go trick-or-treating with you?

Would You Rather...

Scare your friends with a remote-control spider that glows in the dark

with a drone bat that squirts fake blood?

Go to a Halloween party where the guests eat nachos with extra cheese and spider guts

donuts with rainbow sprinkles and witch eyeballs?

Would You Rather...

Go trick-or-treating during a storm that snows fluffy, rainbow-colored marshmallow snowflakes

that pours drippy, white chocolate chip raindrops?

Go to a pizza buffet in a pitch-black cave full of vampire bats

a milkshake bar in a spooky mansion full of funhouse mirrors?

Would You Rather...

Set a world record on Halloween for collecting the most candy in one night

for changing costumes the most times in one night?

Win a trophy for playing ping-pong against a goblin wearing skinny jeans

a medal for playing darts against a zombie wearing a rain poncho?

Would You Rather...

Clone yourself so that your clone can go trick-or-treating in a different costume and collect twice as much candy for you

so that your clone can enter a second costume contest and help you win first place twice?

Boobytrap your candy stash with invisible quicksand

a leaf-covered trap door?

Would You Rather...

Donate your entire treat bag to other kids who didn't get to go trick-or-treating this year

volunteer to make costumes for other kids who don't have one?

Hide your candy in a secret cave at the Grand Canyon

in a treasure chest in the Great Barrier Reef?

Would You Rather...

Learn a magic spell that makes your shadow come to life to help you collect extra treats

that gives you psychic powers to help you locate houses in your neighborhood that give away your favorite candy?

Work at a beauty salon that specializes in painting bumpy witch fingernails

in curling frizzy werewolf hair?

Would You Rather...

Look outside your window on Halloween morning to see a garbage truck transform into a flying robot

to see a zombie mail carrier dropping off packages filled with candy?

Eat pumpkin brownies made with lizard lips and turtle toes

chocolate tarts made with platypus pancreas and llama liver?

Go to a spooky beach to look for silver bullets
with a metal detector

to play frisbee with the Sandman?

Make a Tik Tok video in a rubber chicken costume
with your teacher

take a funny selfie in a video game character costume
with your best friend?

Would You Rather...

Visit a mad scientist's lab to watch sea monkeys grow under a microscope

to observe a mutant frog to study its anatomy?

Design a red and yellow robotic monster costume for a scary movie

a blue and green clown costume for a funny movie?

Would You Rather...

Go to a haunted fair, to ride spinning teacups with a creepy doll who likes cotton candy

jump in a bouncy castle with a two-headed goblin king who likes corndogs?

Make a sculpture of Dracula's castle out of Jell-o

paint a picture of King Tut's pyramid with spray cheese?

Would You Rather...

Dress like an explorer wearing fuzzy bunny slippers and hunt for buried treasure in a pirate cemetery

as an archaeologist wearing goofy mustache glasses and look for hieroglyphics in a mummy's tomb?

Eat tofu pancakes in Bali with a vegan werewolf

candied bacon in Toronto with a carnivorous goblin?

Would You Rather...

Follow scavenger hunt clues that lead you through
a magical bamboo forest to find a pink panda bear costume

through a secret underground cave to find
a red spider costume?

Hide your Halloween candy in a secret compartment
inside your garbage can

in a safe behind your toilet?

Would You Rather...

Go on an African safari on Halloween and see a cheetah wearing pink and green sneakers on its paws

see an albino hippo who likes to swim in chocolate sauce?

Go trick-or-treating while dragging your knuckles on the ground like a gorilla

while walking sideways like a crab?

Would You Rather...

Feed your Halloween candy to giant koi fish who live in an enchanted pond

to tiny mere cats who live in a magic desert habitat?

Have a slumber party at a haunted house where your midnight snack is slimy, peeled grapes that look like lizard eyeballs

gooey, cold spaghetti that feels like monkey brains?

Would You Rather...

Tuck in a colony of baby bats at bedtime by singing them a song about flying under a full moon

by reading them a story about vampires?

Design a robot costume with long, glittery eyelashes for a scary movie about outer space

a clown costume with a man bun for a silly movie about trick-or-treating?

Would You Rather...

Go to the beach with a witch in a bikini who likes to play volleyball

with a vampire in a wet suit who likes to play frisbee?

Play baseball with an ogre who spits pumpkin-flavored sunflower seeds all over the field

play football with a mutant who likes to crush empty soda cans on their forehead?

Would You Rather...

Fly in an airplane sitting next to a lactose-intolerant witch who drinks milk and gets gassy

an annoying ghost who has bad breath and wants to talk the whole flight?

Have a swimming party with a werewolf who can only doggy paddle

with a ghost who only wants to play Marco Polo?

Would You Rather...

Eat as much candy as you want
on Halloween

stay out as late as you want trick-or-treating?

Take a vacation on a haunted cruise ship with a skeleton
crew that likes to perform scenes from your favorite
movie at dinner

with a pirate captain who likes to read your favorite
book before bedtime?

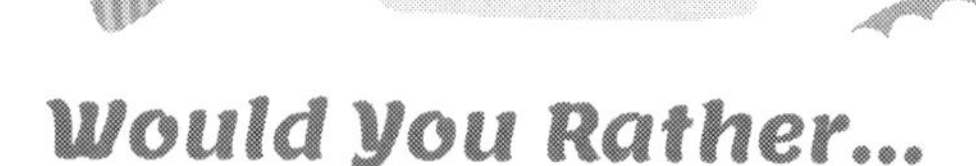

Would You Rather...

Show up to your friend's house to go trick-or-treating on the back of a giant black cat wearing a two-person saddle

in a convertible rocking loud, spooky music?

Go to a birthday party for a mummy with a blue ice cream cake

a birthday party for a zombie with an orange layer cake.

Would You Rather...

Go trick-or-treating for nacho cheese chips that make you sneeze

for fruit punch juice boxes that give you the hiccups?

Have the power to make heavy candy bowls levitate and dump treats into your bag

to summon monsters who dress up with you and give you all their candy?

Would You Rather...

Go wig shopping with a bald werewolf

eat jawbreakers with a toothless vampire?

Have a fort building contest with a swamp creature who has a tractor and wants to build a mud fort

with an owl who has a forklift and wants to build a tree fort?

Would You Rather...

Go trick-or-treating wearing your underwear on your head

your shoes on your hands?

Get an extra treat bag of candy by dressing up as a purple monkey and swinging on vines across the jungle

by dressing up like an orange frog and jumping on lily pads to cross a river?

Would You Rather...

Eat a magic piece of candy that gives you the power to run as fast as a werewolf

the power to jump so high you can touch the moon?

Ride on the back of a motorcycle with a vampire on his way to a biker rally

in a school bus with a zombie basketball team headed to their state playoffs?

Would You Rather...

Play hide and seek with a witch who can teleport to different hiding spots

play dodgeball with a monster who has six arms and a good aim?

Play paintball with a demon while riding on the back of a horse

laser tag with a scarecrow while wearing roller-skates?

Would You Rather...

Go to a slumber party with a scarecrow wearing footie pajamas

to a masquerade ball with a skeleton wearing a hockey mask?

Eat a piece of Halloween candy that you found at the bottom of a dumpster behind the grocery store

that you found on a bathroom floor at a gas station?

Would You Rather...

Have huge buck teeth that stick out of your Halloween mask

long armpit hair that sticks out of your costume sleeves?

Decorate a haunted house on top of a mountain that's shaped like a hexagon

a spooky mansion by the beach that's shaped like a heart?

Would You Rather...

Have a wizard cast a spell on you that gives you super strength

to grow super tall and shrink back down anytime you wanted?

Dress up as a clown with three arms who likes to juggle pumpkins

as a scarecrow with two heads who likes to wear funny hats?

Did You Enjoy The Book ?

If you did, we are ecstatic. If not, please write your complaint to us and we will make ensure we fix it.

If you're feeling generous, there is something important that you can help me with – tell other people that you enjoyed the book.

Ask a grown-up to write about it on Amazon. When they do, more people will find out about the book. It also lets Amazon know that we are making kids around the world laugh. Even a few words and ratings would go a long way.

If you have any ideas or jokes that you think are super funny, please let us know. We would love to hear from you.

Our email address is -

riddleland@riddlelandforkids.com

Riddleland Bonus

Join our **Facebook Group** at **Riddleland for Kids**
to get daily jokes and riddles.

https://pixelfy.me/riddlelandbonus

Thank you for buying this book. As a token of our appreciation, we would like to offer a special bonus—a collection of 50 original jokes, riddles, and funny stories.

CONTEST

Would you like your jokes and riddles to be featured in our next book?

We are having a contest to discover the cleverest and funniest boys and girls in the world!

1) Creative and Challenging Riddles
2) Tickle Your Funny Bone Contest

Parents, please email us your child's "original" riddle or joke. He or she could win a Riddleland book and be featured in our next book.

Here are the rules:

1) We're looking for super challenging riddles and extra funny jokes.

2) Jokes and riddles MUST be 100% original—NOT something discovered on the Internet.

3) You can submit both a joke and a riddle because they are two separate contests.

4) Don't get help from your parents—UNLESS they're as funny as you are.

5) Winners will be announced via email or our Facebook group – **Riddleland for kids**

6) In your entry, please confirm which book you purchased.

Email us at **Riddleland@riddlelandforkids.com**

Other Fun Books by Riddleland

Riddles Series

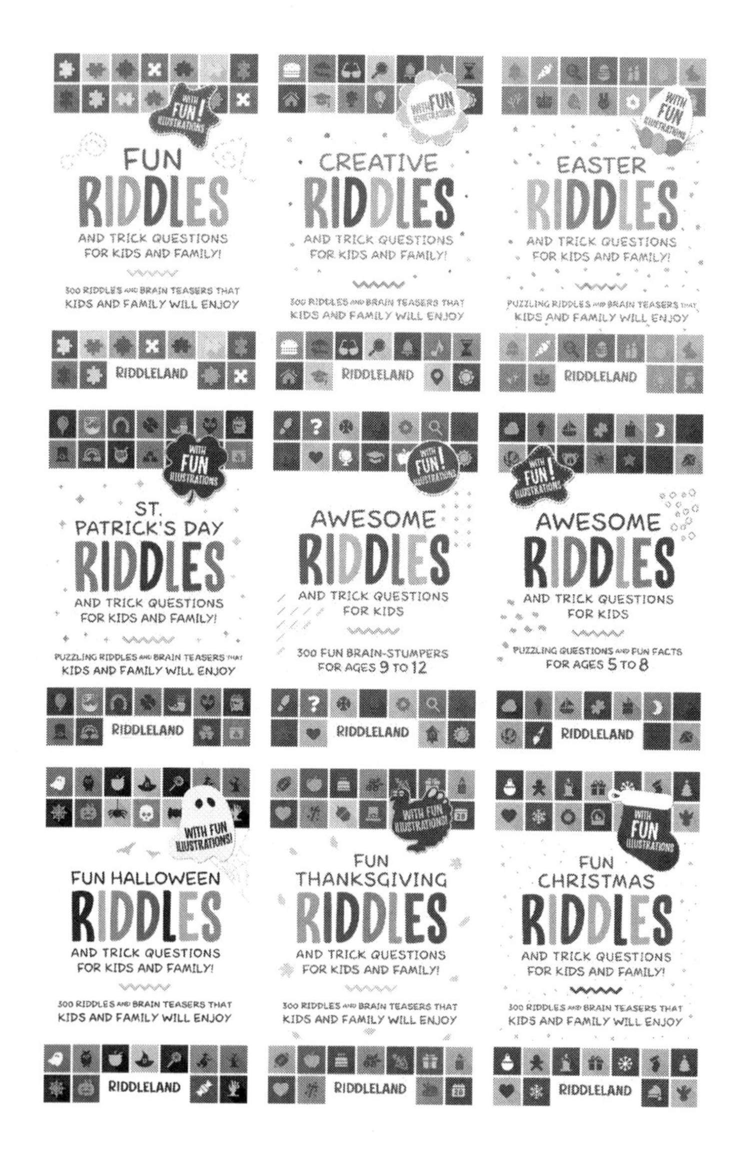

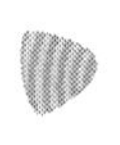

It's Laugh Challenge Would You Rather Books

Get them on Amazon or our website at
www.riddlelandforkids.com

ABOUT RIDDLELAND

Riddleland is a mum + dad run publishing company. We are passionate about creating fun and innovative books to help children develop their reading skills and fall in love with reading. If you have suggestions for us or want to work with us, shoot us an email at

riddleland@riddlelandforkids.com

Our favourite family quote

"Creativity is an area in which younger people have a tremendous advantage since they have an endearing habit of always questioning past wisdom and authority."

– Bill Hewlett

Made in the USA
Middletown, DE
23 September 2021